EGYPT, NUBIA, AND KUSH

BY TONI PAVAN

TABLE OF CONTENTS

Introduction

When we think of **ancient** (AYN-shehnt) Egypt, we think of a land of desert. But ancient Egypt began as a farming community. The land along the Nile was rich and the soil was perfect for farming.

The Egyptians were not the only people to start a **civilization** (siv-uh-lih-ZAY-shuhn) along the Nile River. Farther south, in present-day Sudan, Africa, another civilization had its beginnings in an area known as Nubia.

By about 5500 B.C., people had settled along the lower Nile River. Egypt's great civilization began around 4000 B.C.

Historians do not know exactly when Nubia was first settled. They think it was about 2000 B.C.

Egypt and Nubia had much in common. Both began as farming communities.

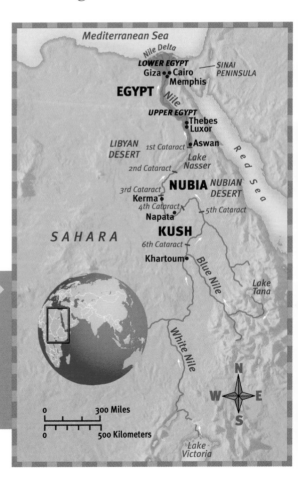

The Nile River flows north and empties into the Mediterranean Sea. The waterfalls, called **cataracts** (KAT-uh-rakts), are numbered from north to south. In ancient times, Nubia was Egypt's neighbor to the south.

Mediterranean Sea
Nile Delta
LOWER EGYPT
Giza • Cairo — SINAI PENINSULA
Memphis
EGYPT Nile
UPPER EGYPT
Thebes
Luxor
LIBYAN DESERT 1st Cataract Aswan
Lake Nasser
2nd Cataract
Red Sea
3rd Cataract NUBIA NUBIAN DESERT
Kerma
4th Cataract
Napata 5th Cataract
SAHARA KUSH
6th Cataract
Khartoum
Blue Nile
Lake Tana
White Nile
N
W E
S
0 300 Miles
0 500 Kilometers
Lake Victoria

Both developed into strong nations. Nubia, later known as Kush, and Egypt would be trading partners at times. Other times, one would be stronger and take control of the other kingdom.

Both kingdoms were **advanced** for their time. They developed centralized governments. They developed into successful agricultural nations. **Artifacts** (AHR-tuh-fakts) from both nations show that each had gifted artisans.

We know more about early Egypt than we do about Nubia. Nubians did not have a written language until much later than Egypt. But since they traded with each other, we have Egyptian records from which we can also learn about ancient Nubia.

Artifacts found in modern-day Sudan, where ancient Nubia was, also reveal an advanced **culture** different than that of Egypt.

↑ **Nubian clay beaker**

↑ **Nubian pendant**

IT'S A FACT

Little was known about the Nubian people until the 1950s. Egypt announced a plan to build a huge dam at Aswan (AH-zwahn). It would block the Nile's flow and create a huge lake. **Archaeologists** (ar-kee-AHL-uh-jihsts) went to work. They dug out Nubian towns and cemeteries. What they found opened a new door to the past.

↑ Early Egyptians were primarily farmers. Slowly, villages grew into cities along the Nile.

Both early civilizations have had an influence on the history of the world, even the world we live in today.

So, sit back and take a sail down the ancient Nile. Learn about two amazing cultures.

Discover the early people of the Nile. Find out what was it like to live there thousands of years ago.

As you read, think about how much our civilization owes to these civilizations of the past.

THE RIVER OF GIFTS

The history of both Egypt and Nubia begins with the Nile River. The mighty Nile is the world's longest river. It is about 4,132 miles (6,650 kilometers) long. Imagine driving across the United States, from California to Georgia, and back again. Now you have an idea of how long the Nile really is!

The Nile flows from south to north. It starts in the mountains of East Africa and empties into the Mediterranean (MEH-dih-teh-RAY-nee-uhn) Sea.

Along the rocky southern part of its route in ancient Nubia, it collects huge rocks. They build up in the water and form six cataracts, or waterfalls.

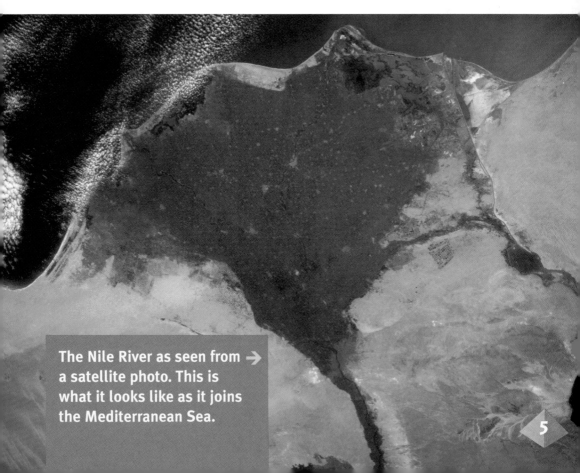

The Nile River as seen from → a satellite photo. This is what it looks like as it joins the Mediterranean Sea.

For thousands of years, the dangerous waterfalls kept invaders out of Nubia.

In the north, the Nile flows smoothly. The river spreads out into a delta. It carries soft black soil, which it leaves before it flows into the sea. The soil in the Nile Delta is very rich, and it is perfect for farming.

IT'S A FACT

Early farmers along the Nile needed a way to collect water from the river's edge, and get it to the farmland. They figured out a way to irrigate their land with something called a shadoof (shuh-DOOF). A bucket was attached to a long pole and used to lift water from the river to land. Shadoofs are still used today along the Nile.

↑ The Nile's second cataract is still a challenge to travelers today.

FLOODS WELCOMED

Starting in spring, the Nile River overflows its banks. The ancient Egyptians knew that this happened every year at the same time. They welcomed the flood. It left behind tons of soil.

Farmers built a series of steps to measure the river's depth. Each step was one cubit high. A cubit was a unit of measure. In a good flood, the Nile would rise sixteen steps.

Around late September, the flooding would end. All along the Nile, ancient farmers planted their crops in the new, wet earth. Crops grew during the warm Egyptian winter. They were harvested before the next flood.

↑ Fish and birds were an important part of the ancient people's diet.

PRIMARY SOURCE

These lines from an ancient Egyptian hymn show how important the Nile River was to the people:

"If the Nile smiles the earth is joyous, every stomach is full of rejoicing."

The ancient Egyptians found ways to deal with the ever-changing Nile. They built mud walls to keep the flood water back. They dug a system of canals (kah-NALZ). The canals carried water to places where the flood didn't reach, like the desert. In time, people had more places to raise food.

↑ The calendar used by the ancient Egyptians was based on the sun.

1. SOLVE THIS

The Nile River empties water into the Mediterranean Sea at 3.1 million liters per second. How many gallons of water empty into the sea in one minute? (One liter equals .2642 gallons.)

MATH ✓ POINT

What strategy did you use to solve this problem?

IT'S A FACT

To keep track of when the flood would come, the ancient Egyptians developed a calendar. It is the oldest calendar based on the sun. It had 365 days, divided into three seasons based on the Nile River's action:

- the flood (beginning of the new year—made land new again)
- land shows after the flood; planting begins
- the harvest

A MAJOR HIGHWAY

The Nile was a water route that allowed people who lived far apart to come together for trade. In ancient Egypt, sailing on the Nile in both directions was possible. For much of the year, the winds blew from north to south. People could go up the river with its flow, and return using sails.

In ancient Nubia, traveling the Nile was very hard. In the south, the river had six cataracts. It was winding.

↑ **The earliest Egyptian boats were made of papyrus (pah-PIGH-ruhs) reeds tied together. By about 3100 B.C., the ancient Egyptians were making large wooden boats for trade and travel. Long oars kept the boat on course.**

THEY MADE A DIFFERENCE

This modern-day boat is made completely of papyrus—just like the boats of early Egypt. In 1970, a Norwegian explorer named Thor Heyerdahl sailed the *Ra II* from Africa to America. He proved that it was possible to sail a boat like this across the Atlantic. No one knows whether any Egyptians ever tried this.

EARLY EGYPT AND NUBIA

The people of early Egypt prospered. Crops grew well as people developed new technologies for farming. There was more food than was needed. This allowed free time for people to develop arts and crafts. Eventually, trade with other cultures began.

The earliest rulers of Egypt were village chiefs. Eventually, two large kingdoms developed. In the Nile Delta was the kingdom of Lower Egypt. In the south, there was Upper Egypt.

Experts believe that King Narmer (NAHR-muhr) united the kingdoms of Egypt into one. He became its first king. Narmer wore the crowns of the two rulers to show respect for both parts of his land.

← All the crowns of pharoahs after Narmer had the head of a cobra in front. It reminded the people that the pharaoh was wise and powerful.

← Narmer's successes were recorded in stone. His story is told in pictures.

IT'S A FACT

Early Egyptians believed that the king was the son of the sun god, Amon-Re, in human form. The king was their link to the gods. Later Egyptians would abandon this idea of the king being a deity.

EGYPTIAN SOCIAL CLASSES

The king made the laws and owned all the land, mines, and water in Egypt. He shared those resources with the people. In turn, they obeyed his commands, and paid taxes (with goods, not money).

Ancient Egyptian society was highly organized. At the head of it was the **pharaoh** (FAIR-oh), or king, and his family. Next in power was the upper class, made up of nobles, priests, and government officials. The officials made sure that the people obeyed the laws and paid their taxes.

Egypt's middle class included small-business owners and artisans. The artists produced linen cloth, jewelry, pottery, and metal goods. Egypt used these items to trade with other civilizations.

The largest group of workers in ancient Egypt were the farmers. Farmers mostly worked land owned by the pharaoh and wealthy nobles.

People who were not farmers and had no special skills were laborers. Some of those people worked along the river, loading and unloading goods from boats. Others worked in the city, making mud bricks for building projects.

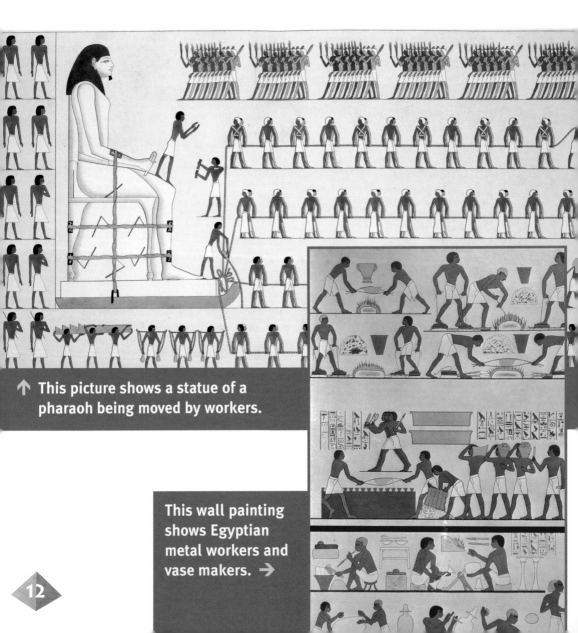

↑ This picture shows a statue of a pharaoh being moved by workers.

This wall painting shows Egyptian metal workers and vase makers. →

LIFE IN EARLY NUBIA

At first, the people of Nubia lived much as the Egyptians did. They traded goods back and forth. Some experts think that the Egyptians might have gotten some of their ideas about religion, government, and way of life from the Nubians. Taking on some of each other's customs and ideas would continue for thousands of years.

↑ The early Nubians made → beautiful clay pottery.

IT'S A FACT

The ancient Egyptian word for gold was *nub*.

13

EARLY WRITING

The ancient Egyptians developed a writing system with more than 700 symbols (SIHM-bulz). Some of the symbols stood for words or ideas. But most stood for sounds. The writing was called **hieroglyphics** (high-eh-ruh-GLIH-fihks).

Some of the most important people in the pharaoh's household were the **scribes** (SKRYBS). They traveled throughout the kingdom to keep records of the harvest. They kept tax records and recorded marriages. It was a great honor to be chosen to become a scribe.

IT'S A FACT

Only boys were allowed to become scribes. Their training began when they were ten years old. They practiced writing first on pieces of broken pottery. Later they learned to write on papyrus.

↑ These labels are some of the earliest samples of Egyptian writing. They help experts understand how the Egyptians developed hieroglyphics.

THEY MADE A DIFFERENCE

The meaning of Egyptian hieroglyphics was lost until the early 1800s when Jean Champollion (ZHON sham-POH-lee-ohn) figured it out. He used a slab of black rock that French soldiers had found in Egypt. On it was old Greek writing and hieroglyphics. Champollion could read Greek. He spent years comparing the Greek words with the hieroglyphics. By 1822, he had cracked the code. The door to understanding life in ancient Egypt was opened.

RELIGION

In early Egypt, the pharaoh was not only a political leader. He was also considered a god.

Egyptians believed that their pharaoh was the child of the sun god Ra. Ancient Egyptians worshipped many gods, but Ra was the most important.

They also believed that when the pharaoh died, he would travel to the "Next World." From there he would continue to help rule Egypt.

The trip to the next world was a long journey. The pharaoh would need many things to help him make the journey. In the afterlife, the pharaoh would need servants, clothing, and jewelry. And he needed a place to be buried with all these things.

But where could all these things be stored? The answer is some of the most amazing structures ever built by man: the **pyramids** (PIHR-uh-midz).

↑ **The pharaoh Akhenatan makes an offering to the sun god.**

MIGHTY BUILDERS

WHAT ARE THE PYRAMIDS?

The Egyptians and Nubians believed in life after death. Burial places were important. They had to be strong and large enough to hold what the person would need in the afterlife. Starting in the Old Kingdom, Egyptian rulers ordered pyramids built as **tombs** (TOOMZ) for themselves and for some family members. Over the next 500 years, more than eighty pyramids were built.

2. SOLVE THIS

The Great Pyramid is 449 feet (137 meters) tall. It is made from about two million blocks of stone, enough to fill a large sports stadium. Some blocks weigh nine tons. The average weight of one block is 2.5 tons. How much does the pyramid weigh?

MATH ✓ POINT

What information do you need to solve the problem?

It took about twenty years to build the Great Pyramid. Under each pyramid are large rooms with paintings and treasures. Each has a long hallway, called the Way of the Sun God, that ends at a secret room where a pharaoh or a family member lay.

The pyramids showed the pharaohs' great wealth and power. Sometimes, the tops of the pyramids were gold. Builders put pyramids in places that were hard to reach. They sealed the pyramids to protect the treasures and the bodies of the pharaohs.

Building a pyramid was not an easy job. A few people were skilled at figuring out what to do and how to do it. But it took thousands of workers to make it happen.

Pyramid builders did not have modern tools or machines. The work was hard and dangerous. Every family had to help. When the Nile floods covered fields, farm families had to work on the pyramids. The cost in human lives and suffering was huge.

Many of the people who dug out the stone for the pyramids were prisoners of war or criminals.

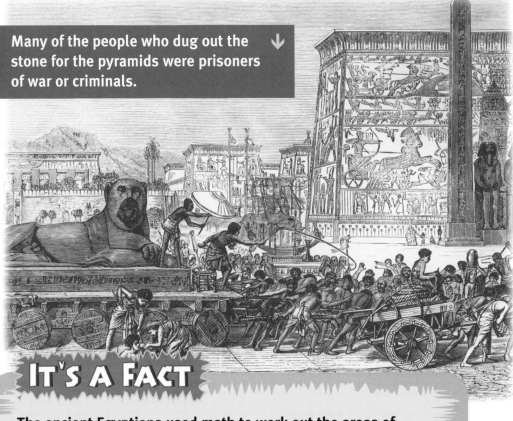

IT'S A FACT

The ancient Egyptians used math to work out the areas of squares, circles, and triangles. They figured out how much land and building supplies they needed. They used a decimal system like ours. They also found a way to deal with fractions.

WHY MUMMIES?

The ancient Egyptians believed that they would need their body in the afterlife. It would be a home for the soul, so it had to stay whole.

The first mummies were probably accidents. In early times, people buried the dead in the sand. Desert sand was hot and dry. Slowly, it took in all the water from the body. The body stayed whole. Later Egyptians found another way to keep their dead.

The ancient Egyptians and Nubians covered the body with a special salt. Then they packed it with leaves, or another dry material, and wrapped it in cloth. The whole process was done in the desert. It took seventy days.

← a mummy and a drawing ↑
of a mummy case

HISTORICAL PERSPECTIVE
THE PYRAMIDS

All through history, people had their own ideas about what the pyramids were. Some thought that they held grain to feed people during hard times. Others thought they stored hidden treasure. Some modern people think that aliens built the pyramids to mark landing places for spaceships! But in the past 100 years, experts have been better able to read hieroglyphics on tomb walls and on papyrus. They also study the actual contents of the tombs. Slowly, we are getting at the truth about the pyramids.

IT'S A FACT

The ancient Egyptians believed that their shadows, as well as their bodies and souls, would go to the afterlife.

LATER EGYPT AND NUBIA

After the Great Pyramid was completed in about 2566 B.C., life in Egypt grew more difficult. The pharaoh collected more taxes to pay for building the pyramids. Over time, people stopped believing that the pharaoh could keep them safe. There was less rain; Nile floods did not bring enough water and rich new earth for farming. The people starved. The pharaoh was no longer a god to his people. Local leaders gained power. By about 2160 B.C., the kingdom had drifted out of the pharaoh's control.

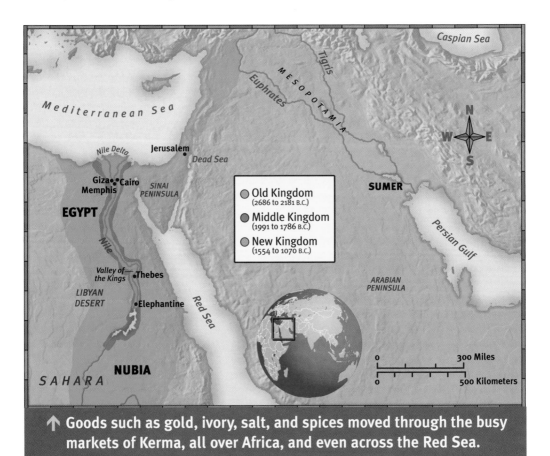

↑ Goods such as gold, ivory, salt, and spices moved through the busy markets of Kerma, all over Africa, and even across the Red Sea.

A POWERFUL NUBIA

While ancient Egypt's troubles grew, the people of Nubia were busy. Around 2400 B.C., they started to form an independent kingdom between Nile cataracts two and four. It was called Kush (KOOSH).

Its capital, Kerma (KAHR-mah), became a big trade center. Some people of Kush became very rich. We know this because of the treasures found in tombs there.

The people of Kush formed their own civilization.

↑ This is one of two ancient deffufas (deh-FOO-fahz) at Kerma. The main temple was inside the city walls.

↑ This sculpture of the god Amun as a ram was made in the New Kingdom.

3. SOLVE THIS

Kerma's main deffufa measures 156 feet by 78 feet (47.5m x 23.8m). Find the perimeter of the defuffa in feet.

MATH ✓ POINT

What steps can you follow to solve the problem?

PRIMARY SOURCE
NUBIAN TREASURES

At Kerma, there are two tall mud brick buildings called deffufas. They were used as temples. The smaller one was the place where prayers and offerings were made for the royals who were buried nearby. Offerings included some amazing treasures: jewelry, carvings, and Egyptian statues of pharaohs and nobles. Experts say the finds prove two things: Kerma's rulers were rich, and the people of Kerma and Egypt were in contact.

NEW RICHES FOR EGYPT

Around 1985 B.C., a time of growth and riches began again in ancient Egypt. A new pharaoh, Amenemhet (AHM-uhn-ehm-het) pulled the country back together and set up a strong central government.

Trade grew. Egypt had more contact with other civilizations. The ancient Egyptians went further into Nubia. They also went to western Asia and returned with such goods as gold, silver, special woods, and new ideas.

The Egyptians moved to take over northern Nubia. They built forts along the Nile. The main job of the troops was to protect the land from a takeover, and protect trade routes.

EXPANSION AND WEALTH

In Egypt, more desert land was prepared for farming. A canal was dug to connect the Nile and the Red Sea. It made trade with western Asia easier.

Around Kush, people continued to trade, farm, and develop their crafts. Experts think that about 2,000 people, including the king, lived and worked in its walled capital, Kerma.

Kush was becoming rich and powerful. Trade goods passed through Kerma. They ended up in markets across the Red Sea and all over Africa.

Reread
Reread page 23. How did Kush become rich and powerful?

↑Traders from Kush brought products from tropical Africa to Kerma: gold, precious wood, animal skins, and giraffe tails.

NEW SETTLERS, NEW RULERS

As trade grew, new peoples began to settle along the Nile. Some of the new settlers came from western Asia. They were called the Hyksos (HIHK-sohs). With the arrival of the new people, many things about life in Egypt changed.

The Hyksos brought new craft skills. They brought horses and chariots (CHA-ree-uhts). The Egyptians learned to ride the horses and drive the chariots.

For a time, the Hyksos became powerful enough to overthrow the pharaoh. They gained control of Lower Egypt and ruled it for more than 150 years.

WHAT HAPPENED?

When the pharaoh Ahmose (AH-mohs) came to power, he was determined to gain back the lands that had been lost to the Hyksos. He vowed that Egypt would never again be ruled by foreigners. His mission was to make Egypt the world's strongest military power.

↑ The Egyptians copied the Hyksos' chariots.

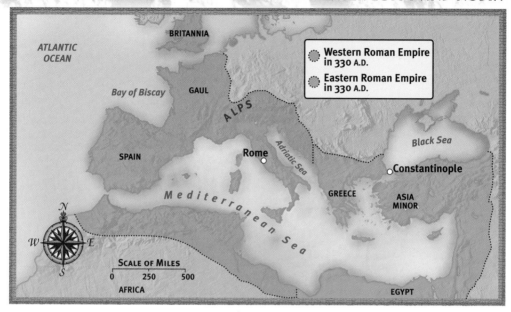

As a result of the success of Ahmose, Egypt became an **empire** (EHM-pighr). We refer to this period of Egyptian history as the New Kingdom.

Egyptian soldiers marched north as far as present-day Israel. Egyptian ships filled with jewelry, linen cloth, and papyrus sailed to Lebanon and Syria.

Egyptians again gained control of Nubia and Kush. This was important because Kush was the gateway to trade with the rest of Africa.

↑ **This Egyptian tomb painting of the loading of grain onto a ship was made around 1450 B.C.**

THEY MADE A DIFFERENCE

Queen Hatshepsut took power after her husband, the pharaoh, died. She ruled for sixteen years. "No one rebels against me," she said. "All foreign (FOR-ihn) lands are my subjects."

Queen Hatshepsut not only made sure that peace was kept throughout her land, she also worked hard to expand Egypt's trade with other lands. One place she wanted to explore was a land called Punt. Historians think Punt may have been in what is today the country of Ethiopia, or maybe Somalia.

A huge caravan of scribes, artists, soldiers, and others set off on the expedition. The trip lasted for two years. When they returned, the travelers brought with them riches from southern Africa including leopard skins, gold, ivory, perfume, and even live apes!

Queen Hatshepsut expanded Egypt's economy through trade with Africa and Asia.

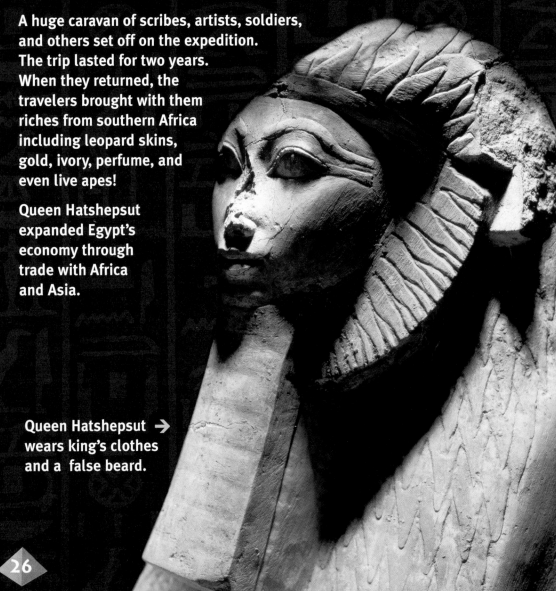

Queen Hatshepsut → wears king's clothes and a false beard.

TRADING IDEAS AND POWER

In the 1400s B.C., Egyptian pharaohs sent troops into Nubia again. This time, Egypt's rule lasted more than 500 years. The people of Kush soaked up Egyptian culture, from beliefs to lifestyles.

Over the next 350 years, power changed hands many times. The capitals of both lands moved. Kush rose and fell again. It invaded Egypt several times. At one time, there were even Kushite pharaohs.

But, around 656 B.C., Kush's control ended forever.

POINT

Read More About It
You can read more about ancient Egypt and Nubia at your school media center or local library. Ask an adult to help you search the Internet for information.

↑ This wall painting shows Tutankamen, an Egyptian pharaoh, and his army fighting Nubians.

IT'S A FACT

By about 730 B.C., Nubian people had learned to write using the Egyptian hieroglyphics. Writing on temple walls, gravestones, and other places gives us a firsthand look at their way of life. It also tells us what the people achieved.

CONCLUSION

The Nile River was very important to the ancient Egyptians and Nubians. No matter where people lived along the river, they had the same concerns about it. The Nile caused people to think up new ideas to control and use the water. They had to work together.

As a result, people developed new ways to bring water to dry land. They figured out when the river would flood, and developed a calendar to keep track of the seasons.

Small farming villages along the Nile grew into large towns and cities. Those places became one kingdom with one ruler, the pharaoh.

Ideas about religion, government, and science developed together, out of need.

As soon as the Egyptians and Nubians discovered each other and began trading, their civilizations influenced each other. Much of their wonderful buildings, art, and writing tells us how they lived, worked, and what they thought. They tell an amazing story of how location and contact affected their rise and fall.

There is still much to find out about the ancient Egyptians and Nubians. Perhaps you will be the archaeologist who digs up some new clues about the ancient Egyptian or Nubian civilizations.

Use this organizer to revisit what you have found out about ancient Egypt and Nubia.

↑ The Nile River helped Egypt and Nubia become rich.

↑ The reasons why Egyptian pharaohs kept power changed after the starving time.

EGYPT, NUBIA, AND KUSH

↑ Contacts between ancient Egypt and Nubia affected the development of both civilizations.

↑ Ancient Egyptians and Nubians had many achievements.

GLOSSARY

advanced   (uhd-VANTSD) ahead of others (page 3)

ancient   (AYN-shehnt) from a time very long ago (page 2)

archaeologist   (ar-kee-AHL-uh-jihst) a scientist who studies the past through the things people have left behind (page 3)

artifact   (AHR-tuh-fakt) something ancient people made by hand that archaeologists find (page 3)

cataract   (KAT-uh-rakt) a waterfall (page 2)

civilization   (siv-uh-lih-ZAY-shuhn) a way of life that a large group of people have developed and organized (page 2)

culture   (KUL-chur) the ways of life, ideas, and arts of a group of people (page 3)

empire   (EHM-pighr) a group of different lands and people governed by the same ruler (page 25)

hieroglyphics   (high-eh-ruh-GLIH-fihks) Egyptian picture writing (page 14)

pharaoh   (FAIR-oh) a ruler of ancient Egypt (page 11)

pyramid   (PIHR-uh-mid) a shape that has a square base and four triangular sides that meet in a point at the top; in ancient Egypt, tombs for pharaohs (page 15)

scribe   (SKRYB) in ancient Egypt, a man who could read and write and whose job was to copy lists, orders, and laws, and keep track of taxes (page 14)

tomb   (TOOM) an underground room used for burial (page 16)

INDEX

SOLVE THIS ANSWERS

1. Page 8
a) 49.14 million gallons (186 million liters)
Math Checkpoint
First multiply 3.1 million liters x 60 seconds to find out how many liters go into the sea in a minute:
3.1 million x 60 seconds = 186 million liters
Then change liters to gallons. One liter equals .2642 gallon.
186 million liters x .2642 gallon = 49.14 million gallons

2. Page 16
5 million tons
Multiply the number of stones times the average weight of each stone.
2,000,000 x 2.5 = 5,000,000 tons
Math Checkpoint
You need to know how many stones were used, and the average weight of each stone.

3. Page 21
468 feet
Math Checkpoint
Perimeter = 2l + 2w
P = (2 x 156 feet) + (2 x 78 feet)
P = (312 feet) + (156 feet)
P = 468 feet or 142.6m
(Based on 1 foot = .3048m)